Loosing
My
Mind

a collection of twenty poems by
Elizabeth Storer

Transparent

Falling
Fell
Deep I delved
No bark just bite
I'm yours tonight
A savage blow
A thief below
To take me there
To take me all

You needn't call
Just whisper dear
I've open heart
And heeding ear
In need of you
I never fear
I join you when
Our bodies near

So meet me when the coast is clear
My soul is yours
I'm always here

Styx

Bones are keepers of the dead
Some are dry and some are wet
I hear them groan beneath my bed
Six feet of soil upon their head

Atop their neck a heavy burden
Rotten wisdom from years of learning
No tongue to lift dead words to ear
If I were them I'd never fear

After I laid them all to rest
A cat's tongue washed my sorrows gone
To their journey I attest
The road is cold and dark and long

XYZ

I lived in hope
Before I was fifteen
They said I could be anything
But it all crashed
Now I'm grown
Everything's for rent
And nothing's owned

Dreaming quickly became unrealistic
If they were handing out guidebooks
Then I must've missed it
And now I'm grown
Just one of many misfits
Thinking about economics

Common Afflictions

A slip of inborn resilience and you don't need to close your eyes
To look on fallow fields in the landscape of our lives
See sought opportunity but like a fish that doesn't bite
We languor in anxiety from overactive fight or flight

Feed it with confectionery, numb with novacaine
Fear like a toothache drills straight into your brain
Beat against the current, make your way up stream
But love isn't the dream it's just a comorbidity

Take your wins and losses and throw them in the bin
They don't mean anything now, the present's all there is
Summon all your courage if you still have fucks to give
If you can do one thing right just know we're made to live

Bookwyrm

Late nights and hunched shoulders
Volumes and tomes to pore over
Dead voices secrets tell
In a trance with childhood spell
The love of reading begins and ends
But you'll return again and again
To the stories of your dreams
To laze in bed is to dance with kings
When tale after tale you bring
In paper bags or tied with string
You're never lonely in your bed
Imagine colours in your head
A dragon vivid red and blue
Or the dingy dusty hue
Of a servants apron too
In the library
With the candlestick
You get your true crime horror fix
Your misty daydreams of days gone by
The woe of lovers cast aside
A victory of highest heights
They come with you to bed at night
And on the train or in the park
You wish you could see in the dark
Then never would their words do part
From your voracious readers heart

gender studies

Yeah it's ok
I didn't want to be alone
I had the heater off but I must have wanted it on
It's amazing how you know me so well
Of course I didn't want you to keep your hands to yourself
And I'm burning up I've got a fever
And your body heat is what I needed
I'm not kicking the blanket off I'm just having trouble covering
my feet
Cus I don't own my body
I have no identity
I don't have needs til you tell me what to need
I really want pizza for the 100th fucking time
Of course babe let's go to bed cus I'm tired
But it's hard to sleep when you're groping me
Did I mention how I'm a million degrees
And I'll just ignore the shooting pain all over my body
So I can lie here and let you do what you want with me
And if I leave the room I know you'll probably just follow me
So I should just give up and get a lobotomy
I don't know why I struggle with my own autonomy
But I know I try to tell you I don't want you on top of me
If I just give up then maybe you'll fall asleep eventually
and I can finally get some peace
Because apparently I don't like the games that I think I like
And if you buy me something then I must think it's nice
I said no when you asked me if I wanted a mountain bike
But you made me pick a colour even though I never ride
I didn't think peer pressure could happen out of school
And if we were there you wouldn't be in my age group
I don't know how last week I was in love with you

But you gave me too much when I wanted less of you
And then you ask me whats wrong like you haven't got a clue
You woke me the fuck up wouldn't that annoy you too
Cus I walk on fucking eggshells so that I never bother you

Bluff

The harbourless harbor
Known for its harsh peaks
Where he crashed his car
Into the night ocean
To stop his heart

The accidents of teenage youth
Left deep scars
But obscure truth
You see it touch them
Look by look

Foolish designs
To organise fools
Key-scratched cars
From childhood feuds

A coastal paradise
Becomes a dystopia
When looked at through
Jaded local eyes

The birds are dead
The sea is dead
The lakes dried up
The sand is red

Custodians

I'll dance with them for the rain
With the smoke
In the sand

Exile from Van Diemen's land
Didn't erase them
Nothing can

Spilling it won't stop their blood
It's in the tree sap
They are our land

We should remember
Kin like these
Their blood is in
The sap of trees

I

In the Sargent's mess
Dine with cloying, inebriating
Honeyed wine
Drink back unstrung nerves
Drink back thoughts of home
A weapon breaking bread
For orders the rich lords gave

Sense of self aside
Whores bed you have made
To be in worshipped glory
While steeped in scorn and shame

Armed with dried up tears
A squatter in the nest
Hides a pointed, iron beak
Up in the leafy rafters
When the bow is loosed
The crow will dive right
Through your open heart

II

The wolves move in
The feeding kin
The danger in the darkness
Warriors of the deepest woods
Whose bark is a harsh laughter
Soft bristling fur caresses oh so sweet
The teeth and claws pick the bones
Slowly of their meat

Raven
Wings as black as night
Perch o'er like a reaper
Watches with impatient delight
Anticipates the feasting
Of little scraps of eyes and tongue
Marrow, muscle, sinew
A dark mortician
Studied well in how he best may eat you

And lower
Far beneath the tree
In the dirt below
The worms and bugs
Will take your filth
And rake it through the soil
Creeping up through the mud
They slither and they crawl
Return you to where you began
The Earth your graceless tomb

Virginity

when I fell
you spoke of moonbeams
carved initials in paperbark trees
a canopy, to kiss beneath the leaves
sparse and wintry

low was the night sky
stars touching our heads
pressing me down into your arms
bodies fusing together
on a park bench

distance grew
in psychological need
while physicality fed
unsatisfied, in satisfying ends
an unfeeling bed

unyielding was attempted
submission was the truth
in a coerced marriage
of giving and taking
confused youth

grieving, a long process
the triumph that preceded
will also follow
i hold my stardust
begin anew

I dream a lot

A knowing ache that we all know too well
A kiss not a kiss but a kiss a spell
Enchanted
Enthralled
You wish for it all
Until you come falling
Teardrops and all

Entangled in wishes
and secret permissions
Hiding in corners
and kissing in cars

Comes in any flavour
Your mystical saviour
Your fantasy man
Just close your eyes

There's something forbidden
in nocturnal emissions
Could be in a castle, a gaol, or bar
Tall dark and handsome will hold you for ransom
As long as you keep lying right where you are

Duet

Dark smile
Glinting eyes
Feeding off of my surprise
Raised eyebrow
Alluring touch
I can't seem to get enough
Seductive whispers
Sweet desire
And I am consumed in his fire

Your warmth stays with me even when you depart
Your voice whispers softly breaking my heart
Your hands are not gentle, they're coarse and they're rough
I want them upon me, leading me on

Prior Learning

It's like there's a wall in front of me
And I can't speak through it
I can't communicate
Because I am petrified

I'm petrified of the words inside
Petrified of tears I will choke on
I was always chastised for showing emotion
Now I'm mute, socially illiterate

I go to therapy to connect the dots
Grieve potential that I lost
Maybe I'm gifted, maybe I'm not
The fact remains I need support

Am I weak for pushing through
How I am
To do what I'm required
When I don't meet the prerequisites

In Absentia

In my sole army bed
With the embrace of dread
I'll walk on with feet of lead
To battlefields I once had fled

I now learn what I didn't know
I weep, I reap in what I sow

The sound shakes the clearing
And the coroner draws near
I can't say I'm just sleeping
I was never really here

She starts monologueing

I find myself adrift in a boat
It has some leaks in it
And I'm afraid it cannot hold my weight
For my heart is a very heavy thing
It hasn't always been
But I'm not sure I like to think about
The times before
The times when I felt whole, content, and unburdened
So I find myself lost in a fog
I cannot recall the last time I saw clearly
Thought clearly
I digress
I have been in this boat alone
It takes something from me
I am missing the lid to my pot
Shut off
Shut up
Shut down
There's nothing here for me
No one there for me
I'm afraid I will be lost
I'm afraid I will crash into the pier
I know not how to stop
Afraid
A life lived incomplete

Bud

I shelter my most tender parts
in a cottage that's not far
that on my back I can carry
and sometimes wear upon my sleeve

The boards are sturdy
The roof is thatched
They sprout like cabbages
In my memory patch

Ideas and dreams
Impractical schemes
When it rains I pluck the weeds
Lest they become my core beliefs

You must tend it
Water and sow
In the fertile soil
Imagination grows

I work on my philosophy
It blooms in form of mother's tree
The apple of her eye I'll be
If the score my body keeps

Sometimes I will try to reach
and prune the overbearing leaves
When they fall to the ground see
the learning that empowers me

In Hindsight

Where'd my seratonin go
I just scroll through my phone
If the wheels don't turn
The car can't go
I'm stalling and no one knows

They can't see and they can't hear
Cus I keep it locked in here
Right behind my closed third eye
Tripping over, running blind

Tell me would it be a crime
If I spent a day alone
I need some form of escape
Books just blur from page to page

Living only in the dark
Daylight doesn't seem to come
It surely must but I don't know
It must be when I'm not around

I'm floating off in space
I'm a hundred thousand ways
To forget this and delay that
Never cleaning up my flat

Live in rubble live in muck
Can't be arsed don't give a fuck
The fucks I don't give smother me
They weigh me down til I can't breathe

Tell me pretty pretty please
Can I make myself some tea
Instead of just going to sleep
I put on weight but I don't eat
Won't speak to friends I only creep

Looking through a pane of glass
The time always goes too fast
A taste of how the others live
Getting married, having kids

Reaching goals and having fun
I could never be someone
To put my unearned guilt aside
When no one cares what I decide

May survive without the drugs
May fuck around and forget love
Make rash decisions
Throw away it all to feel something today

Fan Mail

I've got body envy when your body's close to mine
Could I put you in a blender and drink you up like wine
If I had to live inside you that would suit me fine
Your eyes would be the windows to me on the other side

When I kiss a girl I want our lips to fuse
Crushed petals of velvet, pooling like a bruise
Pushed so hard together, never come apart
When people perceive me I wanna look like art

Untitled

I'm chained to three beds
and two baths
of responsibility
and there's room for everyone
except for me
and the guilt I feel
torn between myself and my family
keeps me from fulfilling either need
I don't know what my house is
with an absence of me
and I'm too scared to leave it
because gender dictates
that it is my duty
but I fail care of
my limited capacity
caused by depression
and ADHD

www.ingramcontent.com/pod-product-compliance
Lightning Source LLC
Chambersburg PA
CBHW022012170726
47994CB00026B/3162